ar Level 5.1/Points 10/Quiz 178111

12 SUPER-GIGANTIC ANIMALS YOU NEED TO KNOW

by Nancy Furstinger

12 STORY LIBRARY

www.12StoryLibrary.com

12-Story Library is an imprint of Peterson Publishing Company and Press Room Editions.

Produced for 12-Story Library by Red Line Editorial

Photographs ©: NightOwlZA/iStockphoto, cover, 1; ChrisKrugerSA/iStockphoto, 4; Johan W. Elzenga/Shutterstock Images, 5; NOAA, 6; Liz Leyden/iStockphoto, 7, 29; Heiko Kiera/Shutterstock Images, 8; Paul Tessier/iStockphoto, 9; Toby Jungen CC 2.0, 10; Lawrence Sawyer/iStockphoto, 11; Rainer von Brandis/iStockphoto, 12; Kristina Vackova/ Shutterstock Images, 13; hacksss/Shutterstock Images, 14; Coica/iStockphoto, 15; pjmalsbury/iStockphoto, 16; Brian Raisbeck/iStockphoto, 17; belu gheorghe/Shutterstock Images, 18; Rey Kamensky/Shutterstock Images, 19; Wildnerdpix/Shutterstock Images, 20; bobby20/Shutterstock Images, 21; TalyaPhoto/Shutterstock Images, 22; DragoNika/ Shutterstock Images, 23, 28; James Michael Dorsey/Shutterstock Images, 24; Leonardo Patrizi/iStockphoto, 25; Rich Lindie/Shutterstock Images, 26; David Osborn/Shutterstock Images, 27

ISBN
978-1-63235-138-8 (hardcover)
978-1-63235-180-7 (paperback)
978-1-62143-232-6 (hosted ebook)

Library of Congress Control Number: 2015934276

Printed in the United States of America
Mankato, MN
June, 2015

Go beyond the book. Get free, up-to-date content on this topic at 12StoryLibrary.com.

TABLE OF CONTENTS

AFRICAN BUSH ELEPHANTS: MIGHTY GIANTS

The African bush elephant is the largest land animal in the world. The tallest elephant ever measured 13 feet (4 m) from its feet to its shoulders. This male weighed 24,000 pounds (10,886 kg). That is approximately the weight of 24 horses.

African elephants' ears are shaped like the continent of Africa.

Most African bush elephants do not grow that large. Bulls, or males, weigh around 14,000 pounds (6,350 kg). Cows, or females, weigh around 7,000 pounds (3,175 kg). Elephants' ears are around one-sixth the size of their

TERRIFIC TUSKS

All elephants have two ivory tusks. These long curved teeth never stop growing. Older bulls can have tusks that measure eight feet (2.4 m) long. The biggest tusks weighed more than 226 pounds (103 kg). Tusks of this size are no longer found on elephants. Poachers have killed the biggest elephants for their ivory.

Calves drink their mother's milk until they are three years old.

bodies. Elephants also have huge brains, bigger than any other land mammal. Their brains weigh between 10 and 12 pounds (4.5 and 5.4 kg).

150,000

Number of muscles in an elephant's trunk.

- Elephants use their trunks to smell, breathe, trumpet, grab, and greet friends.
- An elephant's trunk can grow to seven feet (2.1 m) long.
- Elephants have four molars, each of which can weigh five pounds (2.3 kg).

Besides being enormous, mother elephants also have a longer pregnancy than any other mammal. They can be pregnant for up to 22 months. Newborn elephants are gigantic. A calf weighs approximately 250 pounds (113 kg) at birth. That is around the same size as an adult giant panda. Calves grow quickly from drinking their mother's milk. They gain approximately three pounds (1.4 kg) each day during their first year.

Adult elephants have a giant appetite. They spend 16 hours a day eating food as they roam across Africa's savannas. Adults chow down on approximately 300 pounds (136 kg) of plants each day.

5

BLUE WHALES ARE EARTH'S BIGGEST ANIMAL

The blue whale is the biggest animal that ever lived on Earth. These marine mammals stretch up to 100 feet (30 m) long. That is approximately the length of three school buses. Blue whales can weigh more than 200 tons (181 metric tons). That equals the weight of 2,667 adult humans.

Everything about blue whales is huge. Their tongues weigh nearly 6,000 pounds (2,722 kg), about as heavy as an Asian elephant. Blue whales' hearts are around the size

Blue whales are even larger than the biggest dinosaurs.

and weight of a small car. And some of their blood vessels are so large that a human could swim through them.

Some blue whales raise their tail flukes when they dive down in search of food.

A female blue whale gives birth to a jumbo-sized calf. The 25-foot (7.6-m) calf is born tail first. Calves weigh up to three tons (2.7 metric tons) at birth. They drink 50 gallons (189 L) of their mother's milk each day. That helps them to gain 10 pounds (4.5 kg) per hour. They can put on 250 pounds (113 kg) per day.

Adult blue whales swim the world's oceans. They search for their favorite food: krill. Whales gulp down four tons (3.6 metric tons) of these tiny shrimp-like creatures each day.

9,000
Number of blue whales that remain in oceans.

- A blue whale's tail measures around 25 feet (7.6 m) wide.
- The spout discharged through a blowhole can reach almost 33 feet (10 m) high.
- Blue whales are the loudest animals on Earth and can be noisier than a jet.

THINK ABOUT IT

What gigantic animals once lived on Earth? Why did they go extinct? How might you research the answers to these questions? Think of a way to present the facts you discover to your classmates.

BURMESE PYTHONS GROW TO GREAT LENGTHS

The Burmese python is one of the largest snakes on Earth. A female captive Burmese python named Baby held a world record for her size. Baby lived at the Serpent Safari Park in Illinois. She weighed a hefty 403 pounds (183 kg). That is around the same weight as a male mountain gorilla. Baby measured 27 feet (8.2 m) in length.

Not all Burmese pythons grow this large. Most range from 16 to 23 feet (4.9 to 7 m) in length. Burmese pythons weigh around 200 pounds (91 kg).

Female Burmese pythons grow bigger than males. They are ready to breed once they reach approximately nine feet (2.7 m) long. Females lay up to 100 eggs. The mother snake incubates the eggs for two to three months. She contracts her muscles as she coils around the eggs. When they hatch, baby snakes are 12 to 18 inches (30 to 46 cm) long.

Burmese pythons live in the rain forests of Southeast Asia. They soak up sun during the day. At night they hunt for small mammals and birds. Burmese pythons eat once per week. First they seize their prey using back-curving teeth. The teeth point to the rear to keep prey from

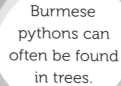

Burmese pythons can often be found in trees.

8

escaping. Then these snakes coil around the prey. They squeeze until the prey suffocates. Finally they swallow their prey whole. Sometimes the meal might be many times larger than the python's head. Pythons stretch their jaws to gulp down their meal.

The female python coils around the eggs to keep them warm.

2,000
Number of invasive Burmese pythons removed from Everglades National Park in Florida.

- Many Burmese pythons found in the Everglades were purchased as 20-inch (51-cm) baby snakes from pet stores and released when they grew.
- The largest python captured in south Florida stretched 18.8 feet (5.7 m).
- American alligators and Burmese pythons engage in deadly battles.

GIANT SALAMANDERS LOOM IN CHINESE LAKES AND STREAMS

The Chinese giant salamander is the largest amphibian in the world. It can grow up to six feet (1.8 m) in length. That is taller than some humans. The tail makes up nearly 60 percent of the body length. The tail can weigh up to 24 pounds (11 kg).

Chinese giant salamanders live in cool streams and lakes in China.

They spend their entire lives in flowing water. Although they have lungs, Chinese giant salamanders take in oxygen from the water through their skin.

Each breeding season, the female lays approximately 500 eggs in an underwater burrow. She leaves after depositing her eggs. Then the

The Chinese giant salamander is known as a living fossil. It has been around for 170 million years.

male guards the eggs for around 60 days until they hatch. The larvae start out tiny. They only measure approximately one inch (2.5 cm) long.

Chinese giant salamanders have poor eyesight. They rely on their senses of touch and smell to hunt. Their skin is covered in nodes. This lets them use vibrations to find prey. The salamanders hide in dark places during the day. Then they hunt for prey at night. When they spot prey, they grip it with their teeth. Then their throat expands and they quickly suck the prey into their mouth. Chinese giant salamanders eat fish, worms, frogs, and toads.

14

Number of nature reserves established for Chinese giant salamander conservation.

- This salamander is critically endangered in China.
- The biggest threat is over-hunting for human consumption.
- A 10-foot (3-m) long salamander was purchased at a local market in the Hunan Province.

Worms are easy for Chinese giant salamanders to find and eat.

COCONUT CRABS SCALE PALM TREES

The coconut crab is the biggest arthropod living on land. These crabs can measure up to three feet (0.9 m) from leg tip to leg tip. Coconut crabs can weigh up to nine pounds (4.1 kg).

This species of hermit crab lives on islands throughout the Indian and Pacific Oceans. The coconut crab climbs palm trees. Then it uses its long, strong pincers to cut down coconuts. Back on the ground, the crab cracks the coconut open and eats the meat inside the shell. The crab also eats other types of fruit and preys on smaller crabs.

Coconut crabs start their life in water. A female crab lays eggs and carries them beneath her abdomen. She waits until the eggs are ready to hatch. Then she releases her eggs into the ocean at high tide. Baby crabs float in the ocean for one

Coconut crabs create a safe burrow in sand.

month. By that time they lose the ability to breathe in water. The crabs search for a discarded mollusk shell, such as a clam. The shell will protect them from predators. The coconut crabs migrate to land. They dig underground burrows in sand or soil. Coconut crabs discard their shells after two or three years when their skin hardens.

50
Number of years a coconut crab can live.

- Coconut crabs can lift weights of up to 62 pounds (28 kg).
- People hunt coconut crabs for their meat, which is considered a delicacy.
- Some islands protect the crabs during their breeding season.

Coconut crabs are strong climbers for their size.

FLEMISH GIANTS MAKE GREAT PETS

The Flemish giant is nicknamed the "king of rabbits." Everything about these pet rabbits is huge. They grow to an impressive size. Darius, the longest Flemish giant on record, stretches out to 4.3 feet (1.3 m) long. He lives in a house in England where he eats off a table and cuddles in laps.

Flemish giants weigh a minimum of 13 to 14 pounds (5.9 to 6.4 kg). By comparison, wild cottontail rabbits weigh between 1.8 and 3.4 pounds (0.81 to 1.5 kg).

These rabbits have big appetites. They chow down on hay and pet rabbit pellets. They also like dark leafy greens and carrots. They nibble apples and bananas.

Female Flemish giants give birth to bunnies after approximately 31 days. The number of bunnies in each litter ranges from five to twelve. Bunnies are born without fur and with their eyes closed. Their eyes open after ten days.

Tame rabbits still have traits of their wild cousins, such as large ears to detect predators. Flemish giants

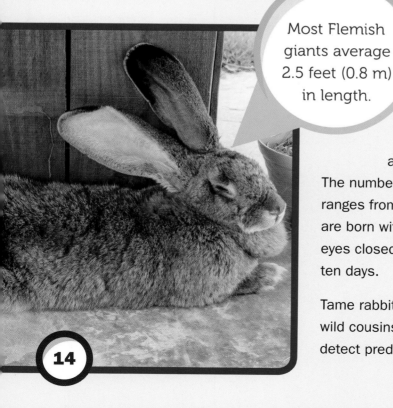

Most Flemish giants average 2.5 feet (0.8 m) in length.

and other pet rabbits usually nap during the day. Then they will explore by hopping around. Sometimes they will jump in the air and twist their head and body in opposite directions.

Flemish giants are most active at dusk and dawn.

1890s
Decade when Flemish giants were first imported into the United States.

- Flemish giants are considered a fancy breed, raised as show rabbits and pets.
- Record holder Darius weighs 50 pounds (23 kg), approximately the size of a medium dog.
- Each day, Darius eats a bowl of rabbit pellets, two apples, a dozen carrots, and half a cabbage.

POPULAR PETS

Flemish giants are gentle and smart rabbits. Unlike some smaller breeds, they are calm. This makes them great pets. Flemish giants are loving companions. They seek out attention. They can be as playful as puppies. These rabbits enjoy being brushed. Their fur comes in seven different colors: black, blue, fawn (a pale yellowish-brown), white, sandy, light gray, and steel gray.

GIRAFFES REACH THE TREETOPS

The giraffe seems to stretch sky-high. This mammal measures 14 to 19 feet (4.3 to 5.8 m) tall. The giraffe's long legs and neck make up most of its height. A giraffe's legs can reach six feet (1.8 m) in length. The neck can extend even longer, around 6.7 feet (2 m). That is the average height of a professional basketball player.

A mother giraffe gives birth standing up. Her calf tucks its head between its front legs. Then it falls more than five feet (1.5 m) to the ground. Within one hour, the six-foot (1.8-m) tall calf can stand on its skinny legs. That same day, it will run alongside its mother.

The giraffe's height gives it many advantages on the savannas of Africa. Long legs allow giraffes to race away from predators. They can move at speeds up to 35 miles per hour (56 km/h). Tall necks let giraffes spot their main predator: the lion. Their height also allows giraffes to reach buds and leaves that grow high above the ground where other animals cannot reach.

However, their height hinders giraffes when they drink water. They have to spread their legs and bend

It can be dangerous for giraffes to bend down to drink water.

9
Number of giraffe subspecies.

- Rothschild giraffes are the most threatened, with fewer than 700 remaining in the wild.
- Similar to human fingerprints, no two giraffes have the same pattern of spots.
- The giraffe's 21-inch (53-cm) tongue is black, blue, or purple.

down. This position makes them vulnerable to predators. It is hard for them to quickly stand up and run. But giraffes do not need water every day. They get most of their water from the plants they eat.

Giraffes can weigh between 1,750 and 2,800 pounds (794 and 1,270 kg).

GREAT DANES STAND TALL

The Great Dane is a massive dog. This breed has earned the nickname "gentle giant." Breed standards state that males should be at least 30 inches (76 cm) tall at the shoulders. Females should measure 28 inches (71 cm) or more at the shoulders.

Two Great Danes won fame for their unusual size. Giant George, who lived in Arizona, held the record as the world's tallest dog from 2010 to 2012. He stood 43 inches (109 cm) at the shoulders. When George stood on his hind legs, he measured 7.3 feet (2.2 m) tall from his nose to his tail. He weighed in at 245 pounds (111 kg). George was about the same height and weight as an African ostrich.

Great Danes are rare in that they do not need a lot of exercise.

6

Number of types of Great Dane coat colors recognized by the American Kennel Club.

- Great Dane coat colors include: black, blue, brindle (yellow with black stripes), fawn, harlequin (white with black patches), and mantle (black and white).
- Great Danes are the only dog breed with a harlequin pattern.
- Like most giant breeds, Great Danes have shorter life spans than smaller dogs, living an average of eight years.

Another famous dog was Zeus in 2013. He beat George's height and length by one inch (2.5 cm). Zeus weighed 165 pounds (75 kg).

Great Danes were first bred in Germany to be tough and strong so they could hunt wild boars. Today, most are kept as family pets. This working breed combines elegance, nobility, and power. The Great

Dane is known for being brave and friendly.

Great Dane puppies grow quickly. They can weigh 100 pounds (45 kg) by the time they are six months old. These giant dogs keep growing until they are around 18 months old.

Great Danes can have several different coat colors.

19

KODIAK BEARS RULE ALASKAN ISLAND

The Kodiak bear is the largest bear in the world. Boars, or males, measure more than 10 feet (3 m) tall when they stand on their hind legs. They can weigh up to 1,500 pounds (680 kg).

Kodiak bears became isolated from mainland bears around 12,000 years ago during the last ice age. They live only on the Kodiak Islands in the Gulf of Alaska. There they eat berries, grass, and plants. They also feast on salmon to prepare for hibernation.

Kodiak bears are much bigger than their brown bear and grizzly bear cousins.

HIBERNATION SECRETS

Kodiak bears can hibernate for up to eight months. During that time, they do not eat or drink. When they emerge from their dens, these bears have not lost bone mass or muscle tone. Scientists are trying to unlock the secrets to how bears achieve these feats. The answers might help patients who are bedridden or paralyzed. It also might help astronauts during long space missions.

Kodiak brown bears hunt for salmon in streams and lakes.

Pregnant sows, or females, are the first to start hibernating in late October. They take cover in dens to conserve energy. They give birth to two or three cubs in January or February. The tiny cubs are born with little fur and closed eyes. The cubs leave their den with their mothers in May or June. Cubs stay with their mothers for three years.

3,500

Population of Kodiak bears on the Kodiak Islands.

- Hunters shot Kodiak bears throughout the 1800s for their hides, which were worth approximately $10 each.
- The 1.9-million-acre (768,900-ha) Kodiak National Wildlife Refuge was created in 1941 to protect the bears' habitat.
- Today 496 permits for Kodiak bear hunting are issued annually.

THINK ABOUT IT

Brainstorm some of the advantages and disadvantages of hibernation. Some scientists describe hibernation as "time migration." Research another animal that hibernates. Then write a story about what happens to this animal during time migration.

MAINE COON CATS ARE A BIG BREED

The Maine coon cat is one of the largest domestic cat breeds. Males can weigh between 13 and 18 pounds (5.9 and 8.2 kg). Females are smaller, weighing between 9 and 13 pounds (4.1 and 5.9 kg). Maine coon cats look even bigger when they are sporting a three-inch (7.6-cm) thick winter coat.

A Maine coon cat named Stewie in Nevada broke records. He held the 2012 record as the world's longest cat. Stewie stretched out to 48.5 inches (123 cm) long. That is the same length as an average seven-year-old child. Stewie also inched his way into the record books for another measurement. This Maine coon held the record for the longest cat tail. His tail measured 16.34 inches (42 cm) long.

No one is sure about the history behind Maine coon cats. Many people believe that this breed started with cats that sailed to early America. Cats were kept aboard ships to hunt rodents. Some cats stayed behind in New England

Maine coon cats are tall and muscular.

and bred with local cats. This breed became the Maine coon.

These cats are named for Maine, where they became the state cat in 1985. They are also named for their ringed tails that look similar to a raccoon's tail. Maine coons are built for cold weather. They use their tails to warm their necks in the winter. Their ears also have tufts of fur on the tips to act as earmuffs.

63
Number of cat breeds recognized by the International Cat Association.

- The Maine coon is one of the oldest natural breeds in North America.
- Some of the first Maine coons were polydactyls, with up to three extra toes on their front paws, hind paws, or both.
- The Maine coon is the second most popular cat breed in the United States. The Persian is number one.

Maine coon cats have tufted paws that act as snowshoes.

OCEAN SUNFISH: TRUCK-SIZED SWIMMERS

The ocean sunfish ranks as the heaviest bony fish in the ocean. These giant fish can weigh up to 5,000 pounds (2,268 kg). That is approximately the weight of a large pickup truck. Their disk-shaped bodies can grow up to 10 feet (3 m) long. Ocean sunfish can measure 14 feet (4.3 m) across from the tip of one fin to the tip of the other.

Ocean sunfish start out tiny. Female sunfish lay millions of eggs. One four-foot (1.2-m) long mother laid more than 300 million eggs. Baby sunfish increase in size 60 million times by the time they are full grown. That is more than any other vertebrate on Earth.

These fish live in temperate and tropical oceans around the world. Ocean sunfish swim slowly, at a top speed of two miles (3.2 km) per hour. Then they dive into deeper waters to hunt for their main prey: jellyfish. Sunfish do not chew their prey. Instead, they suck jellyfish in and out of their tiny mouths. Then they gulp down the small chunks.

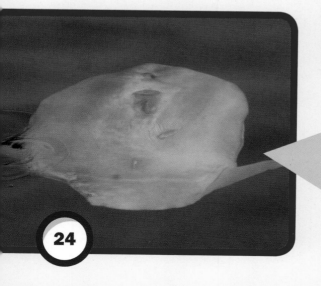

Ocean sunfish sunbathe near the ocean's surface.

An ocean sunfish's back fin folds into itself as the fish grows.

40

Number of times sunfish dive per day.

- In 17th and 18th century Japan, people used sunfish as tax payments.
- Scientists tag sunfish at the base of their dorsal fin to track their movements.
- Ocean sunfish have rough skin and are a silver color.

PESKY PARASITES

Ocean sunfish can become infested with up to 40 kinds of parasites. They need to seek out cleaner fish to nibble off the parasites. Some are too tough for cleaner fish to remove. Then sunfish float to the surface so seagulls can pick off the rest.

SOUTHERN ELEPHANT SEALS LOVE CHILLY WATERS

The southern elephant seal is the largest seal species. Bulls, or males, can top the scales at 8,800 pounds (3,992 kg). Cows, or females, are much smaller. They weigh up to 2,000 pounds (907 kg). Elephant seals do not get their name because of their size. Instead, they are named for their large inflatable noses. Adult males blow up their snouts so they look similar to elephant trunks.

Southern elephant seals spend most of their lives in the chilly Antarctic waters. Bulls fight off rivals. The winner, known as the "beachmaster," might attract up to 100 females. Seal pups weigh approximately 90 pounds (41 kg).

Males use their snouts to make loud roaring noises to attract females.

2

Number of hours that southern elephant seals can remain underwater.

- These seals can dive down more than 4,920 feet (1,500 m).
- They can lower their heart rate to a single beat per minute.
- They spend between 70 and 80 percent of their lives underwater.

Both parent seals lose weight during breeding season, when they fast up to three months. Bulls might lose 40 percent of their body weight. Cows can lose 35 percent of their body weight. Both live off of stored blubber.

RESEARCH ASSISTANTS

Scientists attach minicomputers to the backs of southern elephant seals. The seals help to research the water below the Antarctica sea ice. Computers record data such as how deep the seals dive. Thanks to these seals, scientists discovered that southern oceans appear to be warming faster than other oceans. The minicomputers fall off during the seals' annual molt.

They return to the sea to feast on fish and squid. Elephant seals catch their prey using 30 huge spiky teeth. Then they swallow their prey whole.

Southern elephant seals haul out onto beaches to breed each spring.

FACT SHEET

- Bigger animals are safer from predators because of their size. They also are able to travel farther to search for food. Larger carnivores are in a more favorable position to kill prey, while larger herbivores are able to reach higher foliage. Both are able to store more energy.

- Another plus is that animals with a huge bulk retain heat better so they are less affected by freezing temperatures. They can survive in locations that have big changes in cold and heat because they can effectively monitor their own temperature. Since large animals lose less heat they can survive on lower quality food and digest it over a long time frame to gain nutrition.

- Giant ocean animals do not need enormous skeletons to support their heft. Water, rather than legs, bears most of their weight. Food is more abundant in the ocean. And there are fewer enormous ocean predators.

- Being big also has disadvantages. Larger animals cannot escape danger easily, while smaller species can climb trees, fly away, or burrow below ground. There is more competition for food among giant animals.

- Populations of bigger mammals are more likely to decrease. Generally these mammals are slower to reach breeding age. They are pregnant for a longer amount of time. And they nurse their offspring for longer periods. Their young are at risk of being eaten by predators before they are old enough to breed.

- Large animals generally have shorter life spans than their smaller counterparts. For example, small breed dogs live about 1.5 times longer than large breeds. The colossal Great Dane lives an average of 8.5 years while the tiny Pomeranian lives an average of 15 years.

- Over the ages, many mammals have shrunk in size. But blue whales continue to grow larger. Scientists believe that this growth spurt is due to the increasing amount of krill found in the Southern Ocean surrounding Antarctica.

GLOSSARY

arthropod
An invertebrate animal with jointed limbs, a segmented body, and an external skeleton.

carnivore
A meat eater.

domestic
Kept as a farm animal or pet.

habitat
The place where an animal naturally lives.

haul out
To temporarily leave the water between periods of foraging.

incubate
To sit on eggs and keep them warm until they hatch.

molt
To shed (feathers, hair, or skin) periodically.

node
A protruding knob or lump.

parasite
An organism that lives and feeds off of another organism.

poacher
Someone who hunts and kills an animal illegally.

predator
An animal that preys on others for food.

prey
An animal hunted or killed by another for food.

savanna
A grassland containing scattered trees.

FOR MORE INFORMATION

Books

DK Publishing. *DK Eyewitness Books: Animal.* New York: DK Children, 2012.

Jenkins, Steve. *The Animal Book.* New York: HMH Books for Young Readers, 2013.

Spelman, Lucy. *National Geographic Animal Encyclopedia.* Washington, DC: National Geographic Children's Books, 2012.

Websites

BBC: Supergiant Animals
www.bbc.co.uk/programmes/b03bvxt5

National Geographic: Animals
kids.nationalgeographic.com/animals

National Zoological Park: Animal Records
nationalzoo.si.edu/Animals/AnimalRecords

INDEX

About the Author

Nancy Furstinger has been speaking up for animals since she learned to talk. She is the author of nearly 100 books, including many on her favorite topic: animals! She shares her home with big dogs and house rabbits (all rescued). Furstinger also volunteers for several animal organizations.

Sanibel Public Library